The Science of Mental Health and Well-being

GW00492655

The information provided herein is stated to be truthful and consistent in that any liability, in terms of inattention or otherwise, by any usage or abuse of any policies, processes, or directions contained within is the solitary and utter responsibility of the recipient reader. Under no circumstances will any legal responsibility or blame be held against the publisher for any reparation, damages, or monetary loss due to the information herein, either directly or indirectly.

SCAN ME

Want to receive exclusive updates, promotions, and bonus content related to this book and others, plus the chance to win free books? Look no further! Simply scan the QR code above and enter your email address on the landing page to join our email list.

As a member of our email list, you'll receive:

- Insider information and behind-the-scenes insights
- Special promotions and discounts on future purchases
- Early notification of future book releases

- The chance to win free books through our monthly sweepstakes

Don't wait - scan the QR code and join our email list today for your chance to win!

Table of content

Chapter 1: Introduction to Mental Health and Well-being

Mental health and well-being are essential components of our overall health and happiness. They affect how we think, feel, and behave in our daily lives. Unfortunately, mental health is often stigmatized and misunderstood. This book aims to provide a comprehensive understanding of mental health and well-being, including the latest research, case studies, and strategies for promoting and maintaining mental health and well-being.

Definition of Mental Health and Well-being

Mental health is a state of well-being in which an individual realizes their own abilities, can cope with the normal stresses of life, can work productively and fruitfully, and is able to make a contribution to their community. In contrast, mental illness refers to a wide range of conditions that affect mood, thinking, and behavior. It's important to note that mental health and mental illness exist on a spectrum, and everyone has the potential to experience mental health concerns at some point in their lives.

Well-being, on the other hand, is a holistic concept that encompasses mental, physical, and social well-being. It is about feeling good, functioning well, and having a sense of purpose and meaning in life. It involves not just the absence of illness but also the presence of positive attributes such as happiness, satisfaction, and fulfillment.

Historical Perspectives on Mental Health and Well-being

The understanding and treatment of mental health and well-being have evolved significantly over time. In the past, mental illness was often viewed as a moral failing or a punishment from the gods. Individuals with mental illness were often punished or ostracized. It was not until the 18th century that the first mental hospitals were established, and the treatment of mental illness began to shift towards a more humane approach.

In the 20th century, the field of psychology and psychiatry developed, and new theories and treatments were introduced. The development of psychotherapy and medication revolutionized the treatment of mental illness. However, the stigma surrounding mental health persisted, and individuals with mental illness were still often marginalized and discriminated against.

Today, we have a better understanding of the complex nature of mental health and well-being, and the importance of addressing it as a public health issue. Mental health is now recognized as a fundamental human right, and there is increasing awareness and acceptance of the need for mental health services.

Case Study: John's Journey

John, a 35-year-old man, has struggled with depression for several years. He describes his journey to understanding and improving his mental health. "I always thought that depression was just something that I had to live with," he says. "I didn't realize that there were things I could do to improve my mental health."

Through therapy and medication, John has learned about the causes of his depression and how to manage his symptoms. He has also made lifestyle changes, such as exercising regularly and eating a healthy diet, which have helped improve his mental health. "I feel like I have control over my depression now," he says. "I know that it's something that I'll always have to manage, but I feel like I can live a happy and fulfilling life despite it."

Conclusion

Mental health and well-being are essential components of overall health and happiness. This book aims to provide a comprehensive understanding of mental health and well-being, including the latest research, case studies, and strategies for promoting and maintaining mental health and well-being. By understanding and addressing mental health, we can help break the stigma and discrimination surrounding it, and create a more mentally healthy and inclusive society.

Chapter 2: The Brain and Mental Health

The brain is the most complex organ in the human body and plays a critical role in our mental health and well-being. Understanding how the brain works and how it is related to mental health can provide insight into the causes of mental illness and the potential treatments.

Anatomy and Physiology of the Brain

The brain is divided into several regions, each of which plays a specific role in our mental health and well-being. The cerebrum is the largest part of the brain and is responsible for our conscious thoughts and actions. The cerebellum controls our balance and coordination, while the brainstem controls our vital functions such as breathing and heart rate.

The brain is also divided into several lobes, each of which plays a specific role. The frontal lobes are responsible for our decision-making, problem-solving, and planning. The parietal lobes are responsible for our sensory perception, and the temporal lobes are responsible for our memory and hearing. The occipital lobes are responsible for our vision.

The brain is also made up of various cells, including neurons, which transmit information throughout the brain, and glial cells, which support and protect neurons.

The Role of Neurochemicals in Mental Health

Neurochemicals, also known as neurotransmitters, are chemicals that transmit information between neurons in the brain. These chemicals play a critical role in our mental health and well-being. For example, serotonin is a neurotransmitter that is associated with mood regulation, while dopamine is associated with pleasure and motivation. Imbalance of these neurotransmitters can lead to mental illness.

The Impact of Genetics on Mental Health

Our genes play a significant role in our mental health and well-being. Studies have shown that mental illness tends to run in families, suggesting that there is a genetic component to mental illness. However, it is important to note that genetics are just one factor that contribute to mental illness, and environmental factors also play a significant role.

Case Study: Sarah's Understanding

Sarah, a young woman who has been diagnosed with bipolar disorder, describes how her understanding of her condition has helped her manage her symptoms. "I used to think that my mood swings were just a part of who I am," she says. "But once I understood the biology of my condition, it helped me understand why I was experiencing certain symptoms."

Through therapy and medication, Sarah has been able to better manage her symptoms and lead a more stable life. She also makes sure to take care of her physical and emotional well-being, such as by getting enough sleep, eating a healthy diet, and engaging in regular exercise. By understanding the underlying causes of her condition, Sarah has been able to take a proactive approach to her mental health and improve her overall well-being.

Conclusion

The brain plays a critical role in our mental health and well-being, and understanding how the brain works can provide insight into the causes of mental illness and potential treatments. The brain is made up of various regions and cells, and is influenced by neurochemicals and genetics. By understanding the biology of the brain and mental health, individuals can take a proactive approach to their mental health and improve their overall well-being.

Chapter 3: Stress and Mental Health

Stress is a normal part of life, but when it becomes chronic, it can have a negative impact on our mental health and well-being. Stress can manifest in many ways, such as anxiety, depression, and fatigue, and can lead to physical health problems as well. Understanding the effects of stress on our mental and physical health, and learning effective strategies for managing stress, is essential for maintaining good mental health and well-being.

The Physiological Effects of Stress on the Body

When we experience stress, our body activates the "fight or flight" response, releasing hormones such as adrenaline and cortisol. These hormones help us respond to the stressor by providing a burst of energy, heightened alertness, and increased blood flow to the muscles. However, when stress is chronic, these hormones can have negative effects on the body, such as increasing blood pressure, weakening the immune system, and increasing the risk of heart disease.

The Psychological Effects of Stress on the Mind

Stress can also have a significant impact on our mental health and well-being. It can lead to anxiety, depression, and fatigue, as well as affect our ability to think clearly and make decisions. Chronic stress can also lead to feelings of hopelessness and helplessness, and can make it difficult to cope with everyday challenges.

Strategies for Managing Stress

There are many strategies for managing stress, including:

- Exercise: Regular physical activity can help reduce the effects of stress on the body and mind by releasing endorphins, which are chemicals in the brain that act as natural painkillers and mood elevators.
- Relaxation techniques: Relaxation techniques such as yoga, meditation, and deep breathing can help reduce muscle tension and lower heart rate and blood pressure.
- Time management: Prioritizing and managing time effectively can help reduce the feeling of being overwhelmed by tasks and deadlines.
- Social support: Talking to friends and family, or seeking professional help, can help provide a sense of perspective and support.

Case Study: Mark's Mindfulness

Mark, a high-powered businessman, describes how he has learned to manage stress through mindfulness practices. "I used to be constantly stressed and on edge, but I've learned how to be more present in the moment and focus on my breathing," he says. "It's helped me to not get caught up in the constant chatter in my head."

Mark also makes time for regular exercise and has learned to prioritize and manage his time effectively, which has helped reduce his feeling of being overwhelmed by tasks and deadlines. By implementing these strategies, Mark has been able to reduce his stress levels and improve his overall well-being.

Conclusion

Stress is a normal part of life, but when it becomes chronic, it can have a negative impact on our mental and physical health. The effects of stress on the body and mind can manifest in many ways, such as anxiety, depression, and fatigue. However, by understanding the effects of stress and learning effective strategies for managing stress, individuals can take a proactive approach to their mental health and well-being. This can include regular physical activity, relaxation techniques, time management, and social support. By learning to manage stress, individuals can improve their overall well-being and lead a more balanced and fulfilling life.

Chapter 4: Sleep and Mental Health

Sleep is an essential component of our overall health and well-being. It plays a critical role in physical, mental, and emotional health. Sleep is a time when the body and brain rest and repair, and it is necessary for optimal functioning during the day. Unfortunately, many people struggle with sleep problems, which can have a negative impact on their mental health and well-being.

The Importance of Sleep

During sleep, the brain is able to process and consolidate information, which helps with learning and memory. Sleep also plays a critical role in regulating mood, and lack of sleep can lead to irritability, anxiety, and depression. Furthermore, sleep is essential for physical health, and lack of sleep can increase the risk of chronic health conditions such as obesity, heart disease, and diabetes.

Sleep Disorders

Sleep disorders are common and can have a significant impact on mental health and well-being. Some of the most common sleep disorders include insomnia, sleep apnea, and restless leg syndrome. Insomnia is the most common sleep disorder, and it is characterized by difficulty falling asleep, staying asleep, or both. Sleep apnea is a disorder in which a person's breathing is repeatedly interrupted during sleep, and restless leg syndrome is characterized by an irresistible urge to move the legs.

Strategies for Improving Sleep

There are many strategies for improving sleep, such as:

- Establishing a regular sleep schedule: Going to bed and waking up at the same time every day can help regulate the body's internal clock.

- Creating a sleep-conducive environment: A dark, cool, and quiet room can help promote sleep.
- Relaxation techniques: Relaxation techniques such as yoga, meditation, and deep breathing can help reduce muscle tension and lower heart rate and blood pressure.
- Avoiding electronic devices before bedtime: The blue light emitted by electronic devices can interfere with the production of melatonin, a hormone that regulates sleep.

Case Study: Rachel's Routine

Rachel, a young woman who has struggled with insomnia for years, describes how she has learned to improve her sleep through a combination of relaxation techniques and a regular sleep schedule. "I used to spend hours lying in bed, staring at the ceiling, but now I make sure to establish a regular sleep schedule and do relaxation exercises before bed," she says. "It's made a huge difference in my sleep quality, and I wake up feeling refreshed and energized."

Rachel also avoids electronic devices for at least an hour before bedtime, and creates a sleep-conducive environment in her bedroom. By implementing these strategies, Rachel has been able to improve her sleep quality and reduce her symptoms of anxiety and depression.

Conclusion

Sleep is an essential component of overall health and well-being, and it plays a critical role in physical, mental, and emotional health. Sleep disorders are common and can have a significant impact on mental health and well-being. However, by understanding the importance of sleep, and by learning effective strategies for improving sleep, individuals can take a proactive approach to their mental health and well-being. This can include establishing a regular sleep schedule, creating a sleep-conducive environment, using relaxation techniques, and avoiding electronic devices before bedtime. By learning to improve sleep, individuals can improve their overall well-being and lead a more balanced and fulfilling life.

Chapter 5: Nutrition and Mental Health

Nutrition plays a critical role in our physical and mental health and well-being. The food we eat can affect our mood, energy levels, and cognitive function. Unfortunately, many people have an unbalanced diet, which can have a negative impact on their mental health and well-being. Understanding the relationship between nutrition and mental health, and learning strategies for maintaining a healthy diet, is essential for maintaining good mental health and well-being.

The Relationship between Nutrition and Mental Health

There is a strong relationship between nutrition and mental health. Research has shown that a diet rich in fruits, vegetables, nuts, and fish is associated with lower rates of depression and anxiety. On the other hand, a diet high in processed foods and sugar can increase the risk of depression, anxiety, and other mental health problems.

Nutrients and Mental Health

Certain nutrients are particularly important for mental health and well-being. For example, omega-3 fatty acids, which are found in fish, are important for brain development and function. Vitamin B12 and folate, which are found in leafy greens and nuts, are important for the production of neurotransmitters, which are chemicals in the brain that regulate mood.

Strategies for Maintaining a Healthy Diet

There are many strategies for maintaining a healthy diet, such as:

- Eating a balanced diet: Eating a variety of fruits, vegetables, nuts, and fish can provide the necessary nutrients for mental health and well-being.

- Avoiding processed foods and sugar: Processed foods and sugar can increase the risk of mental health problems.
- Planning ahead: Planning meals and snacks in advance can help ensure that healthy options are always available.
- Seeking professional help: A registered dietitian can provide personalized advice on maintaining a healthy diet.

Case Study: Michael's Meal Planning

Michael, a young man who has struggled with anxiety, describes how he has learned to improve his mental health through a healthy diet. "I used to eat a lot of processed foods and sugar, but I've learned how to plan ahead and make healthier choices," he says. "It's made a huge difference in my mood and energy levels."

Michael now eats a balanced diet that includes a variety of fruits, vegetables, nuts, and fish. He also avoids processed foods and sugar as much as possible. By implementing these strategies, Michael has been able to improve his mental health and overall well-being.

Conclusion

Nutrition plays a critical role in our physical and mental health and well-being. A diet rich in fruits, vegetables, nuts, and fish is associated with lower rates of depression and anxiety, while a diet high in processed foods and sugar can increase the risk of mental health problems. By understanding the relationship between nutrition and mental health and learning strategies for maintaining a healthy diet, individuals can take a proactive approach to their mental health and well-being.

Chapter 6: Exercise and Mental Health

Exercise is an essential component of overall health and well-being. Regular physical activity is not only good for the body, but also has a positive impact on mental health and well-being. Regular exercise can reduce symptoms of anxiety and depression, improve cognitive function, and enhance overall mood. Understanding the relationship between exercise and mental health, and learning strategies for incorporating regular physical activity into one's life, is essential for maintaining good mental health and well-being.

The Relationship between Exercise and Mental Health

There is a strong relationship between exercise and mental health. Regular physical activity has been shown to release endorphins, which are chemicals in the brain that act as natural painkillers and mood elevators. Exercise also helps to regulate stress hormones and improve sleep, both of which are important for mental health and well-being.

Types of Exercise

There are many types of exercise, such as aerobic exercise, strength training, and yoga, each of which have different benefits for mental health. Aerobic exercise, such as running or cycling, can improve cardiovascular fitness and help to reduce symptoms of anxiety and depression. Strength training can help to improve mood and self-esteem, and yoga can help to reduce stress and improve overall well-being.

Strategies for Incorporating Regular Physical Activity

There are many strategies for incorporating regular physical activity into one's life, such as:

- Setting realistic goals: Setting realistic goals, such as walking for 30 minutes a day, can help to make physical activity a part of one's daily routine.
- Finding an activity that one enjoys: Finding an activity that one enjoys, such as dancing or hiking, can make it easier to stick to a regular exercise routine.
- Exercising with a friend or group: Exercising with a friend or group can provide social support and motivation.
- Seeking professional help: A personal trainer or exercise physiologist can provide personalized advice on incorporating regular physical activity into one's life.

Case Study: Susan's Strength Training

Susan, a middle-aged woman who has struggled with depression, describes how she has learned to improve her mental health through strength training. "I used to feel hopeless and helpless, but now I feel strong and empowered," she says. "Strength training has helped me to improve my mood and self-esteem."

Susan now strength trains twice a week and has seen a significant improvement in her mental health. By incorporating regular physical activity into her life, Susan has been able to take a proactive approach to her mental health and improve her overall well-being.

Conclusion

Exercise is an essential component of overall health and well-being, and it has a positive impact on mental health and well-being. Regular physical activity can reduce symptoms of anxiety and depression, improve cognitive function, and enhance overall mood. By understanding the relationship between exercise and mental health and learning strategies for incorporating regular physical activity into one's life, individuals can take a proactive approach to their mental health and well-being.

Chapter 7: Mental Health in Children and Adolescents

Mental health in children and adolescents is an essential aspect of their overall well-being. Mental health problems can develop early on in life and can have a significant impact on a child's development, academic performance and overall quality of life. However, many children and adolescents do not receive the help they need, either due to lack of awareness or stigma. Understanding the mental health needs of children and adolescents, and learning strategies for addressing them, is essential for promoting good mental health and well-being.

Common Mental Health Problems in Children and Adolescents

Children and adolescents can experience a range of mental health problems, such as anxiety, depression, and attention-deficit/hyperactivity disorder (ADHD). These conditions can have a significant impact on a child's academic performance, relationships, and overall well-being.

Risk Factors for Mental Health Problems

There are many risk factors that can increase the likelihood of mental health problems in children and adolescents. These include:

- Genetics: Children with a family history of mental health problems are more likely to develop mental health problems themselves.
- Trauma: Children who have experienced trauma, such as abuse or neglect, are more likely to develop mental health problems.
- Stress: Children who experience high levels of stress, such as from poverty or family conflict, are more likely to develop mental health problems.

Strategies for Addressing Mental Health Problems

There are many strategies for addressing mental health problems in children and adolescents, such as:

- Seeking professional help: A child and adolescent psychiatrist or psychologist can provide specialized treatment and support for mental health problems.
- Family therapy: Family therapy can help to address family dynamics that may be contributing to a child's mental health problems.
- School-based support: Schools can provide support for children and adolescents with mental health problems through counseling, special education, and support groups.
- Supportive community programs: Community programs such as after-school programs and mentoring

can provide support and positive role models for children and adolescents.

Case Study: Tommy's Therapy

Tommy, a ten-year-old boy who has been struggling with anxiety and depression, describes how he has benefited from therapy. "I used to feel really scared and sad, but now I know how to handle my feelings better," he says. "Therapy has helped me to feel more in control of my life."

Tommy's parents also sought family therapy to address family dynamics that may have been contributing to his mental health problems. They also worked with the school to provide Tommy with counseling and special education services. By receiving professional help and support, Tommy has been able to improve his mental health and overall well-being.

Conclusion

Mental health in children and adolescents is an essential aspect of their overall well-being, and mental health problems can develop early on in life. Understanding the mental health needs of children and adolescents, and learning strategies for addressing them, is essential for promoting good mental health and well-being. This can include seeking professional help, family therapy, school-based support, and supportive community programs. By addressing mental health problems early on, we can help children and adolescents lead happier, healthier lives.

Chapter 8: Mental Health in Adults

Mental health in adults is an essential aspect of overall well-being. Mental health problems can develop at any stage of life and can have a significant impact on an individual's relationships, work, and overall quality of life. However, many adults do not receive the help they need, either due to lack of awareness or stigma. Understanding the mental health needs of adults, and learning strategies for addressing them, is essential for promoting good mental health and well-being.

Common Mental Health Problems in Adults

Adults can experience a range of mental health problems, such as anxiety, depression, and post-traumatic stress disorder (PTSD). These conditions can have a significant impact on an individual's work, relationships, and overall well-being.

Risk Factors for Mental Health Problems

There are many risk factors that can increase the likelihood of mental health problems in adults. These include:

- Genetics: Adults with a family history of mental health problems are more likely to develop mental health problems themselves.
- Trauma: Adults who have experienced trauma, such as abuse or a traumatic event, are more likely to develop mental health problems.
- Stress: Adults who experience high levels of stress, such as from work or a relationship, are more likely to develop mental health problems.

Strategies for Addressing Mental Health Problems

There are many strategies for addressing mental health problems in adults, such as:

- Seeking professional help: A psychiatrist or psychologist can provide specialized treatment and support for mental health problems.
- Cognitive-behavioral therapy (CBT): CBT is a form of therapy that can help individuals to change negative patterns of thinking and behavior.
- Medication: Antidepressants and anti-anxiety medication can be effective in treating certain mental health problems.
- Supportive community programs: Community programs such as support groups can provide support and resources for adults with mental health problems.

Case Study: John's Journey

John, a middle-aged man who has been struggling with depression, describes how he has benefited from therapy and medication. "I used to feel hopeless and helpless, but now I have a sense of hope and control," he says. "Therapy has helped me to understand my feelings better, and the medication has helped to reduce my symptoms."

John also sought support from a community program, and found it helpful to talk with others who have shared similar experiences. By receiving professional help and support, John has been able to improve his mental health and overall well-being.

Conclusion

Mental health in adults is an essential aspect of overall well-being, and mental health problems can develop at any stage of life. Understanding the mental health needs of adults, and learning strategies for addressing them, is essential for promoting good mental health and well-being. This can include seeking professional help, cognitive-behavioral therapy, medication, and supportive community programs. By addressing mental health problems early on, adults can lead happier, healthier lives.

Chapter 9: Mental Health and Substance Abuse

Mental health and substance abuse are closely related issues that can have a significant impact on an individual's overall well-being. Substance abuse can lead to the development of mental health problems, and mental health problems can lead to an increased risk of substance abuse. Understanding the relationship between mental health and substance abuse, and learning strategies for addressing both, is essential for promoting good mental health and well-being.

The Relationship between Mental Health and Substance Abuse

There is a complex relationship between mental health and substance abuse. Substance abuse can lead to the development of mental health problems, such as depression and anxiety, and mental health problems can lead to an increased risk of substance abuse. For example, individuals who experience high levels of stress or trauma may turn to drugs or alcohol as a way to cope with their feelings. On the other hand, individuals with mental health problems such as depression or anxiety may be more likely to abuse drugs or alcohol as a way to self-medicate.

Common Substances of Abuse

There are many different substances that can be abused, including:

- Alcohol: Alcohol is a legal substance that can be abused and can lead to addiction.
- Opioids: Opioids are a class of drugs that can be prescribed for pain relief, but can also be abused and lead to addiction.

- Stimulants: Stimulants, such as cocaine and methamphetamine, can be abused and lead to addiction.
- Benzodiazepines: Benzodiazepines are a class of drugs that can be prescribed for anxiety, but can also be abused and lead to addiction.

Treatment for Substance Abuse and Mental Health

Treatment for substance abuse and mental health typically involves a combination of therapy, medication, and support groups.

- Therapy: Therapy can help individuals to understand the underlying causes of their substance abuse and mental health problems, and to develop coping strategies.
- Medication: Medication can be used to help individuals to overcome addiction and to treat underlying mental health problems.

- Support groups: Support groups can provide a supportive environment where individuals can share their experiences and receive support from others who are going through similar struggles.

Case Study: Karen's Story

Karen, a young woman who has struggled with substance abuse and depression, describes how she has benefited from treatment. "I used to feel like I was stuck in a cycle of addiction and depression, but now I feel like I have a chance at a better life," she says. "Treatment has helped me to understand the underlying causes of my problems, and to develop coping strategies."

Karen received therapy and medication for her substance abuse and depression. She also found support groups to be helpful in her recovery. By receiving treatment for both her substance abuse and mental health problems, Karen has been able to improve her overall well-being.

Conclusion

Mental health and substance abuse are closely related issues that can have a significant impact on an individual's overall well-being. Substance abuse can lead to the development of mental health problems, and mental health problems can lead to an increased risk of substance abuse. Understanding the relationship between mental health and substance abuse, and learning strategies for addressing both, is essential for promoting good mental health and well-being. This can include therapy, medication, and support groups. By addressing both mental health and substance abuse, individuals can lead happier, healthier lives.

Chapter 10: Mental Health and Physical Health

Mental health and physical health are closely related and can have a significant impact on an individual's overall well-being. Physical health can affect mental health, and mental health can affect physical health. Understanding the relationship between mental health and physical health, and learning strategies for promoting overall health and well-being, is essential for good mental health and well-being.

The Impact of Physical Health on Mental Health

Physical health can have a significant impact on mental health. Chronic physical conditions, such as heart disease or diabetes, can increase the risk of developing mental health problems, such as depression or anxiety. Physical health problems can also exacerbate existing mental health problems, making it harder for individuals to manage their symptoms.

The Impact of Mental Health on Physical Health

Mental health can also have a significant impact on physical health. Mental health problems, such as depression or anxiety, can increase the risk of developing chronic physical conditions, such as heart disease or diabetes. Mental health problems can also exacerbate existing physical health problems, making it harder for individuals to manage their symptoms.

Strategies for Promoting Overall Health and Well-being

There are many strategies for promoting overall health and well-being, such as:

- Holistic approach: A holistic approach to health care that addresses both physical and mental health can be effective in promoting overall health and well-being.

- Regular check-ups: Regular check-ups with a primary care physician can help to identify physical health problems early on and address them before they become chronic conditions.
- Mind-body therapies: Mind-body therapies, such as yoga or meditation, can be effective in promoting overall health and well-being by addressing both physical and mental health.

Case Study: A primary care physician, Dr. Smith, describes how they helped a patient with chronic pain improve their mental health through a holistic approach. The patient, who had been struggling with depression and anxiety, was referred to a therapist for counseling and started practicing yoga as a form of mind-body therapy. By addressing both the patient's physical and mental health, Dr. Smith was able to help the patient improve their overall health and well-being.

Conclusion

Mental health and physical health are closely related and can have a significant impact on an individual's overall well-being. Physical health can affect mental health, and mental health can affect physical health. Understanding the relationship between mental health and physical health, and learning strategies for promoting overall health and well-being, is essential for good mental health and well-being. This can include a holistic approach, regular check-ups, and mind-body therapies. By addressing both mental health and physical health, individuals can lead happier, healthier lives.

Chapter 11: Mental Health and Relationships

Mental health and relationships are closely related and can have a significant impact on an individual's overall well-being. Relationships can affect mental health, and mental health can affect relationships. Understanding the relationship between mental health and relationships, and learning strategies for promoting positive relationships and well-being, is essential for good mental health and well-being.

The Impact of Relationships on Mental Health

Relationships can have a significant impact on mental health. Positive relationships, such as with friends and family, can provide social support and improve mental health. On the other hand, negative relationships, such as those marked by conflict or abuse, can worsen mental health and increase the risk of developing mental health problems.

The Impact of Mental Health on Relationships

Mental health can also have a significant impact on relationships. Mental health problems, such as depression or anxiety, can make it harder for individuals to form and maintain positive relationships. Mental health problems can also exacerbate existing relationship problems, making it harder for individuals to resolve conflicts or build trust.

Strategies for Promoting Positive Relationships and Well-being

There are many strategies for promoting positive relationships and well-being, such as:

- Communication: Good communication is essential for

building and maintaining positive relationships.

- Boundaries: Setting healthy boundaries can help to improve relationships by reducing conflict and promoting respect.
- Empathy: Showing empathy and understanding towards others can help to build trust and positive relationships.
- Seeking professional help: A therapist can provide specialized treatment and support for relationship problems and mental health issues.

Case Study: A couple, Jane and Michael, who have been struggling with communication and trust issues in their relationship, describe how they have benefited from therapy. Through therapy, they have learned to communicate more effectively, set healthy boundaries, and show empathy towards one another. By addressing their relationship problems and mental health issues, they have been able to improve their overall well-being.

Conclusion

Mental health and relationships are closely related and can have a significant impact on an individual's overall well-being. Relationships can affect mental health, and mental health can affect relationships. Understanding the relationship between mental health and relationships, and learning strategies for promoting positive relationships and well-being, is essential for good mental health and well-being. This can include effective communication, setting boundaries, empathy, and seeking professional help. By addressing relationship problems and mental health issues, individuals can lead happier, healthier lives.

Chapter 12: Mental Health and the Workplace

Mental health and the workplace are closely related and can have a significant impact on an individual's overall well-being. The workplace can affect mental health, and mental health can affect the workplace. Understanding the relationship between mental health and the workplace, and learning strategies for promoting positive mental health in the workplace, is essential for good mental health and well-being.

The Impact of the Workplace on Mental Health

The workplace can have a significant impact on mental health. Factors such as job stress, lack of job control, and job insecurity can increase the risk of developing mental health problems, such as depression or anxiety. Workplace culture and the support provided by employers and colleagues can also affect mental health.

The Impact of Mental Health on the Workplace

Mental health can also have a significant impact on the workplace. Mental health problems, such as depression or anxiety, can affect an individual's ability to perform their job, leading to decreased productivity and increased absenteeism. Mental health problems can also affect an individual's ability to form and maintain positive relationships with colleagues.

Strategies for Promoting Positive Mental Health in the Workplace

There are many strategies for promoting positive mental health in the workplace, such as:

- Employee Assistance Programs (EAPs): EAPs can provide employees with confidential counseling and support for mental health and personal issues.

- Workplace Wellness Programs: Workplace wellness programs can promote healthy behaviors and reduce the risk of developing mental health problems.
- Supportive Management: Managers who provide support and understanding can help to reduce job stress and improve mental health.
- Creating a positive workplace culture: Encouraging open communication, promoting work-life balance, and fostering a culture of inclusivity and respect can also help to promote positive mental health in the workplace.
- Training and education: Providing training and education on mental health, stress management, and effective coping strategies can help employees to better understand and manage their mental health.

Case Study: A company, XYZ Ltd, has implemented a workplace wellness program which includes regular employee surveys to assess mental health and well-being, and an Employee Assistance Program (EAP) that provides counseling and support for employees. The program has been successful in reducing stress and improving the mental health of employees, leading to increased productivity and job satisfaction.

Conclusion

Mental health and the workplace are closely related and can have a significant impact on an individual's overall well-being. The workplace can affect mental health, and mental health can affect the workplace. Understanding the relationship between mental health and the workplace, and learning strategies for promoting positive mental health in the workplace, is essential for good mental health and well-being. This can include Employee Assistance Programs (EAPs), Workplace Wellness Programs,

Supportive Management, creating a positive workplace culture, and providing training and education on mental health. By addressing mental health in the workplace, employees can lead happier, healthier lives and companies can benefit from increased productivity and job satisfaction.

Chapter 13: Mental Health and Technology

Mental health and technology are closely related and can have a significant impact on an individual's overall well-being. Technology can affect mental health, and mental health can affect technology use. Understanding the relationship between mental health and technology, and learning strategies for promoting positive mental health in relation to technology, is essential for good mental health and well-being.

The Impact of Technology on Mental Health

Technology can have a significant impact on mental health. The constant accessibility and use of technology can lead to increased stress, social isolation, and decreased sleep quality. It can also increase the risk of developing mental health problems such as depression and anxiety.

The Impact of Mental Health on Technology Use

Mental health can also affect technology use. Mental health problems, such as depression or anxiety, can lead to excessive use of technology as a form of self-soothing or escapism. This can lead to further deterioration of mental health and difficulty in managing the symptoms.

Strategies for Promoting Positive Mental Health in relation to Technology

There are many strategies for promoting positive mental health in relation to technology, such as:

- Digital Detox: Setting aside time to disconnect from technology can help to reduce stress and improve mental health.
- Mindful Use: Using technology mindfully and being aware of its

impact on one's mental health can help to reduce negative effects.

- Balancing Online and Offline life: Finding a balance between online and offline life by setting limits on technology use can help to improve mental health.
- Seeking professional help: A therapist or counselor can provide specialized treatment and support for technology addiction and mental health issues related to technology use.

Case Study: A teenager, Tom, who has been struggling with depression and social isolation, has found relief by setting limits on his technology use and finding a balance between online and offline life. He has also sought professional help and has been able to improve his mental health by addressing his technology addiction and underlying mental health issues.

Conclusion

Mental health and technology are closely related and can have a significant impact on an individual's overall well-being. Technology can affect mental health, and mental health can affect technology use. Understanding the relationship between mental health and technology, and learning strategies for promoting positive mental health in relation to technology, is essential for good mental health and well-being. This can include Digital Detox, Mindful Use, Balancing Online and Offline life, and seeking professional help. By addressing technology addiction and underlying mental health issues, individuals can lead happier, healthier lives with better mental well-being.

Chapter 14: Mental Health and Spirituality

Mental health and spirituality are closely related and can have a significant impact on an individual's overall well-being. Spirituality can affect mental health, and mental health can affect spirituality. Understanding the relationship between mental health and spirituality, and learning strategies for promoting positive mental health in relation to spirituality, is essential for good mental health and well-being.

The Impact of Spirituality on Mental Health

Spirituality can have a significant impact on mental health. For some individuals, spirituality can provide a sense of meaning and purpose, which can improve mental health. Spirituality can also provide a sense of connection to something greater than oneself, which can promote a sense of well-being and reduce stress.

The Impact of Mental Health on Spirituality

Mental health can also affect spirituality. Mental health problems, such as depression or anxiety, can make it harder for individuals to connect with their spirituality and find meaning and purpose. Mental health problems can also affect an individual's ability to participate in spiritual practices and rituals.

Strategies for Promoting Positive Mental Health in relation to Spirituality

There are many strategies for promoting positive mental health in relation to spirituality, such as:

- Mindfulness Practices: Mindfulness practices, such as meditation, can help to reduce stress and improve mental health.

- Connection to Nature: Spending time in nature can help to promote a sense of well-being and reduce stress.
- Spiritual Practices: Engaging in spiritual practices, such as prayer or yoga, can help to improve mental health.
- Seeking professional help: A therapist or counselor who is trained in spiritual practices can provide specialized treatment and support for mental health issues related to spirituality.

Case Study: A young woman, Mary, who has been struggling with anxiety and depression has found relief by incorporating mindfulness practices and spiritual practices such as yoga and meditation into her daily routine. She has also found comfort in nature and been able to improve her mental health by addressing her underlying mental health issues and connecting with her spirituality.

Conclusion

Mental health and spirituality are closely related and can have a significant impact on an individual's overall well-being. Spirituality can affect mental health, and mental health can affect spirituality. Understanding the relationship between mental health and spirituality, and learning strategies for promoting positive mental health in relation to spirituality, is essential for good mental health and well-being. This can include mindfulness practices, connection to nature, spiritual practices, and seeking professional help. By addressing underlying mental health issues and connecting with spirituality, individuals can lead happier, healthier lives with better mental well-being.

Chapter 15: Mental Health and Culture

Mental health and culture are closely related and can have a significant impact on an individual's overall well-being. Culture can affect mental health, and mental health can affect culture. Understanding the relationship between mental health and culture, and learning strategies for promoting positive mental health in relation to culture, is essential for good mental health and well-being.

The Impact of Culture on Mental Health

Culture can have a significant impact on mental health. Culture can shape an individual's beliefs, values, and attitudes towards mental health, which can affect how mental health issues are perceived and addressed. Culture can also influence the types of treatments and therapies that are considered appropriate for mental health issues.

The Impact of Mental Health on Culture

Mental health can also affect culture. Mental health problems, such as depression or anxiety, can make it harder for individuals to participate in cultural practices and rituals. Mental health problems can also affect an individual's ability to maintain cultural connections and relationships.

Strategies for Promoting Positive Mental Health in relation to Culture

There are many strategies for promoting positive mental health in relation to culture, such as:

- Cultural competence: Understanding and respecting the cultural beliefs, values, and attitudes of individuals can help to promote positive mental health.

- Cultural sensitivity: Being sensitive to the cultural needs of individuals can help to reduce stress and improve mental health.
- Cultural identity: Maintaining cultural identity can help to promote a sense of well-being and reduce stress.
- Seeking professional help: A therapist or counselor who is trained in cultural competency can provide specialized treatment and support for mental health issues related to culture.

Case Study: A young man, Ahmed, who has been struggling with depression and anxiety, has found relief by reconnecting with his cultural heritage and participating in cultural practices such as traditional dances and festivals. He has also sought professional help from a therapist trained in cultural competency, who has helped him to understand and address the cultural factors affecting his mental health.

Conclusion

Mental health and culture are closely related and can have a significant impact on an individual's overall well-being. Culture can affect mental health, and mental health can affect culture. Understanding the relationship between mental health and culture, and learning strategies for promoting positive mental health in relation to culture, is essential for good mental health and well-being. This can include cultural competence, cultural sensitivity, cultural identity, and seeking professional help. By addressing cultural factors affecting mental health and maintaining cultural connections, individuals can lead happier, healthier lives with better mental well-being.

Chapter 16: Mental Health and Gender

Mental health and gender are closely related and can have a significant impact on an individual's overall well-being. Gender can affect mental health, and mental health can affect gender. Understanding the relationship between mental health and gender, and learning strategies for promoting positive mental health in relation to gender, is essential for good mental health and well-being.

The Impact of Gender on Mental Health

Gender can have a significant impact on mental health. Gender can shape an individual's experiences, beliefs, and attitudes towards mental health, which can affect how mental health issues are perceived and addressed. Gender can also influence the types of treatments and therapies that are considered appropriate for mental health issues.

The Impact of Mental Health on Gender

Mental health can also affect gender. Mental health problems, such as depression or anxiety, can make it harder for individuals to express their gender identity and participate in gender-affirming activities. Mental health problems can also affect an individual's ability to maintain healthy relationships and engage in social activities.

Strategies for Promoting Positive Mental Health in relation to Gender

There are many strategies for promoting positive mental health in relation to gender, such as:

- Gender-affirming therapy: Gender-affirming therapy can help individuals to explore and express their gender identity.

- Supportive and inclusive environments: Creating supportive and inclusive environments can help to reduce stress and improve mental health.
- Advocacy and activism: Engaging in advocacy and activism can help to improve social attitudes towards gender and mental health.
- Seeking professional help: A therapist or counselor who is trained in gender-affirming therapy can provide specialized treatment and support for mental health issues related to gender.

Case Study: A young trans man, Alex, who has been struggling with depression and anxiety, has found relief by participating in gender-affirming therapy and exploring his gender identity. He has also found support in a trans-inclusive community and been able to improve his mental health by addressing the social and cultural factors affecting his mental health.

Conclusion

Mental health and gender are closely related and can have a significant impact on an individual's overall well-being. Gender can affect mental health, and mental health can affect gender. Understanding the relationship between mental health and gender, and learning strategies for promoting positive mental health in relation to gender, is essential for good mental health and well-being. This can include gender-affirming therapy, supportive and inclusive environments, advocacy and activism, and seeking professional help. By addressing gender-related factors affecting mental health and promoting gender-inclusivity, individuals can lead happier, healthier lives with better mental well-being.

It is also important to note that research suggests that individuals who identify as transgender, non-binary, or gender non-conforming experience higher rates of mental health issues such as depression, anxiety, and suicide. Therefore, it is crucial that healthcare professionals and society as a whole become more educated and sensitive to the unique needs and experiences of individuals who identify as transgender, non-binary, or gender non-conforming in order to promote better mental health and well-being for these individuals.

In addition, it is important to recognize that each individual's experience with their gender identity is unique and that there is no one "right" way to express or explore one's gender identity. Therefore, it is important to approach each individual with an open mind and provide a safe and non-judgmental space for them to explore and express their gender identity.

In conclusion, by understanding the relationship between mental health and gender, and by promoting gender-affirming therapy, supportive and inclusive environments, advocacy and activism, and seeking professional help, individuals can lead happier, healthier lives with better mental well-being. By promoting inclusivity, education and understanding, society as a whole can contribute to better mental health and well-being for individuals of all gender identities.

Chapter 17: Mental Health and Sexual Orientation

Mental health and sexual orientation are closely related and can have a significant impact on an individual's overall well-being. Sexual orientation can affect mental health, and mental health can affect sexual orientation. Understanding the relationship between mental health and sexual orientation, and learning strategies for promoting positive mental health in relation to sexual orientation, is essential for good mental health and well-being.

The Impact of Sexual Orientation on Mental Health

Sexual orientation can have a significant impact on mental health. Individuals who identify as lesbian, gay, bisexual, transgender, or queer (LGBTQ+) may face discrimination, stigma, and social marginalization, which can affect their mental health. These experiences can lead to increased rates of mental health issues such as depression, anxiety, and suicide.

The Impact of Mental Health on Sexual Orientation

Mental health can also affect sexual orientation. Mental health problems, such as depression or anxiety, can make it harder for individuals to express their sexual orientation and participate in activities that align with their sexual orientation. Mental health problems can also affect an individual's ability to maintain healthy relationships and engage in social activities.

Strategies for Promoting Positive Mental Health in relation to Sexual Orientation

There are many strategies for promoting positive mental health in relation to sexual orientation, such as:

- LGBTQ+-affirming therapy: LGBTQ+-affirming therapy can help individuals to explore and express their sexual orientation.
- Supportive and inclusive environments: Creating supportive and inclusive environments can help to reduce stress and improve mental health.
- Advocacy and activism: Engaging in advocacy and activism can help to improve social attitudes towards sexual orientation and mental health.
- Seeking professional help: A therapist or counselor who is trained in LGBTQ+-affirming therapy can provide specialized treatment and support for mental health issues related to sexual orientation.

Case Study: A young gay man, David, who has been struggling with depression and anxiety, has found relief by participating in LGBTQ+-affirming therapy and exploring his sexual orientation. He has also found support in a LGBTQ+-inclusive community and been able to improve his mental health by addressing the social and cultural factors affecting his mental health.

Conclusion

Mental health and sexual orientation are closely related and can have a significant impact on an individual's overall well-being. Sexual orientation can affect mental health, and mental health can affect sexual orientation. Understanding the relationship between mental health and sexual orientation, and learning strategies for promoting positive mental health in relation to sexual orientation, is essential for good mental health and well-being. This can include LGBTQ+-affirming therapy, supportive and inclusive environments, advocacy and activism, and seeking professional help. By addressing the discrimination, stigma, and marginalization that individuals who identify as LGBTQ+

may face, and by promoting inclusivity, education and understanding, society as a whole can contribute to better mental health and well-being for individuals of all sexual orientations.

It is also important to note that research suggests that individuals who identify as LGBTQ+ experience higher rates of mental health issues such as depression, anxiety, and suicide. Therefore, it is crucial that healthcare professionals and society as a whole become more educated and sensitive to the unique needs and experiences of individuals who identify as LGBTQ+ in order to promote better mental health and well-being for these individuals.

In addition, it is important to recognize that each individual's experience with their sexual orientation is unique and that there is no one "right" way to express or explore one's sexual orientation. Therefore, it is important to approach each individual with an open mind and provide a safe and non-judgmental space for them to explore and express their sexual orientation.

In conclusion, by understanding the relationship between mental health and sexual orientation, and by promoting LGBTQ+-affirming therapy, supportive and inclusive environments, advocacy and activism, and seeking professional help, individuals can lead happier, healthier lives with better mental well-being. By promoting inclusivity, education and understanding, society as a whole can contribute to better mental health and well-being for individuals of all sexual orientations.

Chapter 18: Mental Health and Trauma

Mental health and trauma are closely related and can have a significant impact on an individual's overall well-being. Trauma can affect mental health, and mental health can affect an individual's ability to cope with and process trauma. Understanding the relationship between mental health and trauma, and learning strategies for promoting positive mental health in relation to trauma, is essential for good mental health and well-being.

The Impact of Trauma on Mental Health

Trauma can have a significant impact on mental health. Trauma, such as experiencing a natural disaster, physical or sexual abuse, or experiencing a traumatic event, can lead to the development of mental health issues such as post-traumatic stress disorder

(PTSD), depression, and anxiety. These experiences can also lead to increased rates of substance abuse, self-harm, and suicide.

The Impact of Mental Health on Trauma

Mental health can also affect an individual's ability to cope with and process trauma. Mental health problems, such as depression or anxiety, can make it harder for individuals to process their experiences and move forward from a traumatic event. Mental health problems can also affect an individual's ability to maintain healthy relationships and engage in social activities.

Strategies for Promoting Positive Mental Health in relation to Trauma

There are many strategies for promoting positive mental health in relation to trauma, such as:

- Trauma-focused therapy: Trauma-focused therapy can help

individuals to process their experiences and move forward from a traumatic event.

- Supportive and inclusive environments: Creating supportive and inclusive environments can help to reduce stress and improve mental health.
- Seeking professional help: A therapist or counselor who is trained in trauma-focused therapy can provide specialized treatment and support for mental health issues related to trauma.

Case Study: A young woman, Alice, who has been struggling with depression and PTSD after experiencing sexual abuse, has found relief by participating in trauma-focused therapy. She has also found support in a supportive community and been able to improve her mental health by addressing the social and cultural factors affecting her mental health.

Conclusion

Mental health and trauma are closely related and can have a significant impact on an individual's overall well-being. Trauma can affect mental health, and mental health can affect an individual's ability to cope with and process trauma. Understanding the relationship between mental health and trauma, and learning strategies for promoting positive mental health in relation to trauma, is essential for good mental health and well-being. This can include trauma-focused therapy, supportive and inclusive environments, and seeking professional help. By addressing the impact of trauma on mental health and promoting inclusivity and understanding, society as a whole can contribute to better mental health and well-being for individuals who have experienced trauma.

Chapter 19: Mental Health and Resilience

Mental health and resilience are closely related and can have a significant impact on an individual's overall well-being. Resilience can affect mental health, and mental health can affect an individual's ability to cope with stress and adversity. Understanding the relationship between mental health and resilience, and learning strategies for promoting positive mental health and resilience, is essential for good mental health and well-being.

The Impact of Resilience on Mental Health

Resilience can have a significant impact on mental health. Individuals who are resilient are better able to cope with stress and adversity, which can lead to better mental health outcomes. Resilience can also help to reduce the risk of developing mental health issues such as depression and anxiety.

The Impact of Mental Health on Resilience

Mental health can also affect an individual's ability to be resilient. Mental health problems, such as depression or anxiety, can make it harder for individuals to cope with stress and adversity. Mental health problems can also affect an individual's ability to maintain healthy relationships and engage in social activities.

Strategies for Promoting Positive Mental Health and Resilience

There are many strategies for promoting positive mental health and resilience, such as:

- Building resilience: Building resilience can help individuals to cope with stress and adversity, which can lead to better mental health outcomes.

- Supportive and inclusive environments: Creating supportive and inclusive environments can help to reduce stress and improve mental health.
- Mindfulness and meditation: Mindfulness and meditation can help individuals to be more resilient by reducing stress and promoting a sense of well-being.
- Seeking professional help: A therapist or counselor can provide specialized treatment and support for mental health issues and help individuals build resilience.

Case Study: A young man, Jack, who has been struggling with depression and anxiety after losing his job, has found relief by building his resilience through mindfulness and meditation practices, seeking professional help and participating in a support group for people who are unemployed. He has also found support in a supportive community and been able to improve his mental health by addressing the social and cultural factors affecting his mental health.

Conclusion

Mental health and resilience are closely related and can have a significant impact on an individual's overall well-being. Resilience can affect mental health, and mental health can affect an individual's ability to cope with stress and adversity. Understanding the relationship between mental health and resilience, and learning strategies for promoting positive mental health and resilience, is essential for good mental health and well-being. This can include building resilience, supportive and inclusive environments, mindfulness and meditation, and seeking professional help. By promoting resilience and addressing the impact of stress and adversity on mental health, society as a whole can contribute to better mental health and well-being for individuals.

Chapter 20: Mental Health and Public Policy

Mental health and public policy are closely related and can have a significant impact on an individual's overall well-being. Public policy can affect mental health, and mental health can affect an individual's ability to access and navigate the healthcare system. Understanding the relationship between mental health and public policy, and learning strategies for promoting positive mental health through public policy, is essential for good mental health and well-being.

The Impact of Public Policy on Mental Health

Public policy can have a significant impact on mental health. Government policies that provide access to mental health services, such as funding for mental health research and support for community mental health programs, can help to improve mental health outcomes. However, policies that limit access to mental health services, such as cuts to funding for mental health programs, can have a negative impact on mental health.

The Impact of Mental Health on Public Policy

Mental health can also affect public policy. Individuals with mental health issues may require specific policies, such as accommodations in the workplace, to help them to manage their mental health problems. Mental health can also affect an individual's ability to access and navigate the healthcare system.

Strategies for Promoting Positive Mental Health through Public Policy

There are many strategies for promoting positive mental health through public policy, such as:

- Providing access to mental health services: Government policies that provide access to mental health services, such as funding for mental health research and support for community mental health programs, can help to improve mental health outcomes.
- Addressing the social determinants of mental health: Government policies that address the social determinants of mental health, such as poverty and discrimination, can help to improve mental health outcomes.
- Encouraging mental health literacy: Government policies that encourage mental health literacy, such as education and awareness campaigns, can help to reduce the stigma associated with mental health and improve access to mental health services.
- Promoting research: Government policies that promote research can help to improve our understanding of

mental health and develop new and effective treatments.

Case Study: A young woman, Emma, who has been struggling with anxiety and depression, has found relief by accessing mental health services through a government-funded community mental health program. She has also found support in a supportive community and been able to improve her mental health by addressing the social and cultural factors affecting her mental health.

Conclusion

Mental health and public policy are closely related and can have a significant impact on an individual's overall well-being. Public policy can affect mental health, and mental health can affect an individual's ability to access and navigate the healthcare system. Understanding the relationship between mental health and public policy, and learning strategies for promoting positive mental health through public policy, is essential for good mental health and well-being. This can include providing access to mental health services, addressing the social determinants of mental health, encouraging mental health literacy and promoting research. By promoting effective public policy, society as a whole can contribute to better mental health and well-being for individuals.

Chapter 21: Mental Health and the Media

Mental health and the media are closely related and can have a significant impact on an individual's overall well-being. The media can affect mental health, and mental health can affect an individual's ability to navigate and interpret the information presented in the media. Understanding the relationship between mental health and the media, and learning strategies for promoting positive mental health through the media, is essential for good mental health and well-being.

The Impact of the Media on Mental Health

The media can have a significant impact on mental health. The way that mental health is portrayed in the media can affect how individuals perceive and understand mental health. Negative stereotypes and misinformation in the media can contribute to the stigma associated with mental health and prevent individuals from seeking help. On the other hand, accurate and positive representation of mental health in the media can help to reduce the stigma and increase awareness of mental health issues.

The Impact of Mental Health on the Media

Mental health can also affect the media. Individuals with mental health issues may be more vulnerable to the negative effects of the media, such as increased anxiety or depression. Mental health can also affect an individual's ability to navigate and interpret the information presented in the media.

Strategies for Promoting Positive Mental Health through the Media

There are many strategies for promoting positive mental health through the media, such as:

- Encouraging responsible and accurate representation of mental health in the media: Encouraging media outlets to present accurate and positive representations of mental health can help to reduce the stigma associated with mental health and increase awareness of mental health issues.
- Providing education and resources for the media: Providing education and resources for media outlets can help to ensure that mental health is accurately represented in the media.
- Encouraging media literacy: Encouraging individuals to develop media literacy skills can help them to navigate and interpret the information presented in the media in a healthy and positive way.

Case Study: A young man, John, who has been struggling with anxiety and depression, has found relief by developing media literacy skills and becoming more critical of the representation of mental health in the media. He has also found support in a supportive community and been able to improve his mental health by addressing the social and cultural factors affecting his mental health.

Conclusion

Mental health and the media are closely related and can have a significant impact on an individual's overall well-being. The media can affect mental health, and mental health can affect an individual's ability to navigate and interpret the information presented in the media. Understanding the relationship between mental health and the media, and learning strategies for promoting positive mental health through the media, is essential for good mental health and well-being. This can include encouraging responsible and accurate representation of mental health in the media, providing education and resources for the media, and encouraging media literacy. By promoting positive representation of mental health in the media, society as a whole can contribute to reducing the stigma associated with mental health and increasing awareness and access to mental health services for individuals. It is important for individuals to be aware of the media's influence on mental health and to develop the skills to critically evaluate and make sense of the information they encounter in the media.

Chapter 22: Mental Health and the Arts

Mental health and the arts are closely related and can have a significant impact on an individual's overall well-being. The arts can affect mental health, and mental health can affect an individual's ability to engage and participate in the arts. Understanding the relationship between mental health and the arts, and learning strategies for promoting positive mental health through the arts, is essential for good mental health and well-being.

The Impact of the Arts on Mental Health

The arts can have a significant impact on mental health. Engaging in the arts, such as painting, music, or theatre, can help to reduce stress, improve mood, and promote well-being. The arts can also be used as a form of therapy, helping individuals to process and express difficult emotions.

The Impact of Mental Health on the Arts

Mental health can also affect an individual's ability to engage and participate in the arts. Mental health issues, such as depression or anxiety, can make it harder for individuals to engage in creative activities and can affect an individual's ability to express themselves through the arts.

Strategies for Promoting Positive Mental Health through the Arts

There are many strategies for promoting positive mental health through the arts, such as:

- Engaging in creative activities: Engaging in creative activities, such as painting, music, or theatre, can help to reduce stress, improve mood, and promote well-being.

- Using the arts as therapy: Using the arts as a form of therapy can help individuals to process and express difficult emotions.
- Encouraging access to the arts: Encouraging access to the arts, such as through community art programs, can help individuals to engage in creative activities and promote well-being.
- Building community through the arts: Building community through the arts can help to promote social connections and support networks.

Case Study: A young woman, Sarah, who has been struggling with depression and anxiety, has found relief by engaging in a community art program and using the arts as a form of therapy. She has also found support in a supportive community and been able to improve her mental health by expressing herself through the arts and building connections with other individuals in the program. Through the arts, she has been able to find new ways of coping with her mental health issues and has been able to improve her overall well-being.

Conclusion

Mental health and the arts are closely related and can have a significant impact on an individual's overall well-being. The arts can affect mental health, and mental health can affect an individual's ability to engage and participate in the arts. Understanding the relationship between mental health and the arts, and learning strategies for promoting positive mental health through the arts, is essential for good mental health and well-being. This can include engaging in creative activities, using the arts as therapy, encouraging access to the arts, and building community through the arts. The arts can provide an avenue for self-expression and help individuals to cope with mental health issues and improve overall well-being.

Chapter 23: Mental Health and the Future

Mental health and the future are closely related and it is important to consider the impact of current and future societal and technological developments on mental health and well-being. Understanding the potential challenges and opportunities related to mental health in the future is essential for promoting good mental health and well-being for all individuals.

Potential Challenges for Mental Health in the Future

There are several potential challenges for mental health in the future, such as:

- The impact of technology: The increasing use of technology, such as social media and smartphones, can have a negative impact on mental health, leading to increased stress, anxiety, and depression.

- Climate change: Climate change can have a negative impact on mental health, leading to increased stress, anxiety, and depression.
- Economic inequality: Economic inequality can lead to increased stress, anxiety, and depression.

Potential Opportunities for Mental Health in the Future

There are also several potential opportunities for mental health in the future, such as:

- Advancements in technology: Advancements in technology can be used to improve mental health, such as through virtual reality therapy and teletherapy.

- Increased awareness and understanding of mental health: Increased awareness and understanding of mental health can lead to more effective prevention and treatment of mental health issues.
- Increased access to mental health services: Increased access to mental health services, such as through teletherapy, can help to improve mental health and well-being for all individuals.

Case Study: A young woman, Emma, who has been struggling with anxiety and depression, has found relief through virtual reality therapy and teletherapy. She has also found support in a supportive community and been able to improve her mental health by addressing the social and technological factors affecting her mental health.

Conclusion

Mental health and the future are closely related and it is important to consider the impact of current and future societal and technological developments on mental health and well-being. There are potential challenges, such as the impact of technology and climate change, but also potential opportunities, such as advancements in technology and increased awareness and access to mental health services. By understanding the potential challenges and opportunities related to mental health in the future, we can work towards promoting good mental health and well-being for all individuals.

Chapter 24: Conclusion and Next Steps

Mental health and well-being are essential for leading a fulfilling life, and it is important to understand the various factors that can impact mental health and well-being. The Science of Mental Health and Well-being has explored key concepts and issues related to mental health and well-being, including the brain and mental health, stress and mental health, sleep and mental health, nutrition and mental health, exercise and mental health, mental health in children and adolescents, mental health in adults, mental health in older adults, mental health and substance abuse, mental health and physical health, mental health and relationship, mental health and work, mental health and technology, mental health and spirituality, mental health and culture, mental health and gender, mental health and sexual orientation, mental health and trauma, mental health and resilience, mental health and public policy, mental health and the media, mental health and the arts, and mental health and the future.

The Importance of Understanding Mental Health and Well-being

Understanding mental health and well-being is important for promoting good mental health and well-being. By understanding the various factors that can impact mental health and well-being, individuals can take steps to improve their mental health and well-being.

Next Steps

There are several next steps that can be taken to promote good mental health and well-being, such as:

- Encouraging responsible and accurate representation of mental health in the media: Encouraging media outlets to present accurate and positive representations of mental health can help to reduce the stigma associated with mental health and increase awareness of mental health issues.

- Providing education and resources for the media: Providing education and resources for media outlets can help to ensure that mental health is accurately represented in the media.

- Encouraging media literacy: Encouraging individuals to develop media literacy skills can help them to navigate and interpret the information presented in the media in a healthy and positive way.

- Encouraging access to the arts: Encouraging access to the arts, such as through community art programs, can help individuals to engage in creative activities and promote well-being.

- Building community through the arts: Building community through the arts can help to promote social connections and support networks.

- Encouraging access to mental health services: Encouraging access to mental health services, such as through teletherapy, can help to improve mental health and well-being for all individuals. This can include increasing funding for mental health services, reducing barriers to access such as cost and lack of transportation, and promoting awareness of mental health services and their benefits.
- Promoting overall health and well-being: Promoting overall health and well-being, including physical, emotional and spiritual health, can help to improve mental health and well-being. This can include promoting healthy lifestyle choices, such as regular exercise, healthy eating, and good sleep hygiene.
- Advocating for mental health in public policy: Advocating for mental health in public policy can help to improve mental health and well-being

for all individuals. This can include advocating for increased funding for mental health services, promoting mental health awareness and education, and reducing barriers to access mental health services.

Conclusion

Mental health and well-being are essential for leading a fulfilling life, and it is important to understand the various factors that can impact mental health and well-being. There are several next steps that can be taken to promote good mental health and well-being, including encouraging responsible and accurate representation of mental health in the media, providing education and resources for the media, encouraging media literacy, encouraging access to the arts, building community through the arts, encouraging access to mental health services, promoting overall health and well-being, and advocating for mental health in public policy. By taking these steps, we can work towards improving mental health and well-being for all individuals.

Printed in Great Britain
by Amazon